D0186792

Maths
made easy

Key Stage 1
Ages 5-6
Advanced

Author Sue Phillips, Linda Ruggieri
Consultant Sean McArdle

Congratulations to ....
for successfully finishing this book.

(write your name here)

☆ *You're a star!* ☆

Numbers

Which numbers are the snakes hiding?
Look, and say them as you write.

1	2	3	4	5		7	8	
11			14	15		17		19	20
21	22		24	25		27	28		30
	32	33	34	35		37	38	
41		44	45	46			49	50

9 | 10

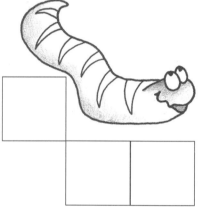

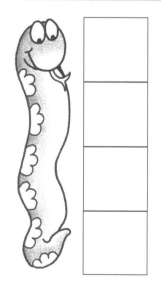

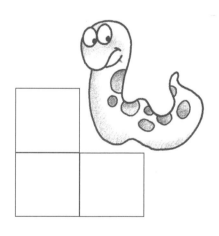

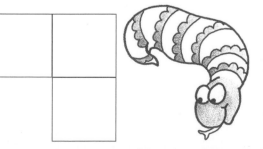

1 less or 1 more

Count, draw, and write.

1 less   1 more
1 less   54 55 56 57 1 more 58

1 less 61 1 more

1 less 79 1 more

1 less 98 1 more

1 less 17 1 more

1 less 50 1 more

Counting in 2s

Draw in the hops and write in the numbers.
Do you need to add or take away?

24   +2   26   +2   28   +2   30   +2   32

37   −2   35   −2   33   −2   31   −2   29

48   −2

43   +2

32   +2

21   −2

43   −2

Counting in 3s, 4s, and 5s

Draw in the arrows and write the numbers on the toadstools.
Do you need to add or take away?

Row 1: 20 +3 23 +3 26 +3 29 +3 32 +3 35

Row 2: 20 −3

Row 3: 30 −4

Row 4: 26 −5

Row 5: 17 +4

Row 6: 21 +5

5

Patterns of 2, 5, and 10

Count, colour, and find a pattern.

Count in 2s and colour them red.

1	2	3	4	5	6	7	8	9	10
11	12	13	14	15	16	17	18	19	20
21	22	23	24	25	26	27	28	29	30
31	32	33	34	35	36	37	38	39	40
41	42	43	44	45	46	47	48	49	50

Count in 5s and colour them purple.

1	2	3	4	5	6	7	8	9	10
11	12	13	14	15	16	17	18	19	20
21	22	23	24	25	26	27	28	29	30
31	32	33	34	35	36	37	38	39	40
41	42	43	44	45	46	47	48	49	50

Count in 10s and colour them yellow.

1	2	3	4	5	6	7	8	9	10
11	12	13	14	15	16	17	18	19	20
21	22	23	24	25	26	27	28	29	30
31	32	33	34	35	36	37	38	39	40
41	42	43	44	45	46	47	48	49	50

More or less

Link the spaceships to the planets, and the rockets to the stars.

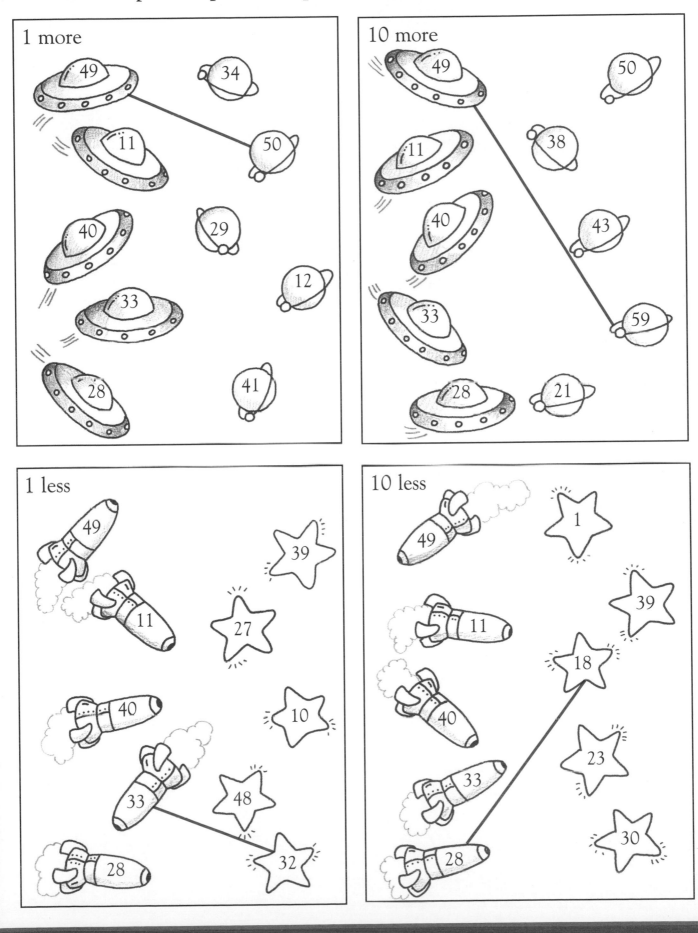

Fractions of numbers

Draw a ring round the objects that make up the fractions and write the missing numbers.

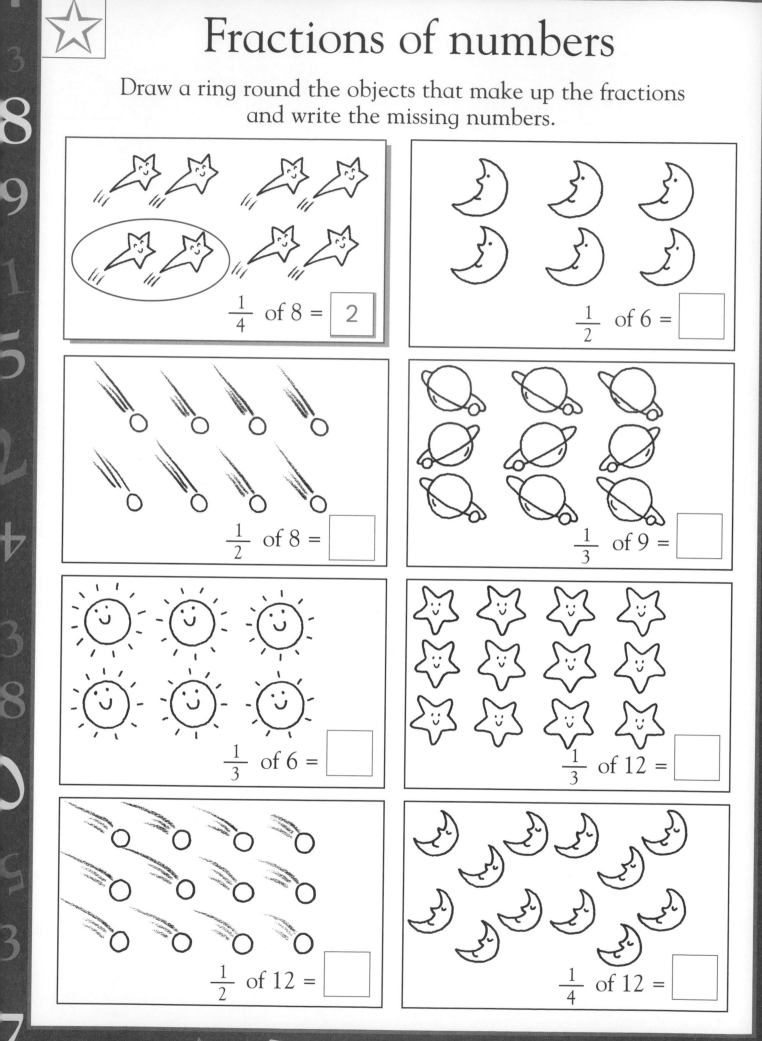

$\frac{1}{4}$ of 8 = 2

$\frac{1}{2}$ of 6 = ☐

$\frac{1}{2}$ of 8 = ☐

$\frac{1}{3}$ of 9 = ☐

$\frac{1}{3}$ of 6 = ☐

$\frac{1}{3}$ of 12 = ☐

$\frac{1}{2}$ of 12 = ☐

$\frac{1}{4}$ of 12 = ☐

Adding grid

Draw rings round the pairs of numbers that add up to 20.

15	5	3	10	10	4	19
8	6	20	0	9	1	10
12	13	7	12	0	16	1
4	5	10	16	4	5	10
9	2	18	7	20	3	10
11	3	3	1	0	11	9
17	1	1	19	3	18	11

Doubles

Write the missing numbers.

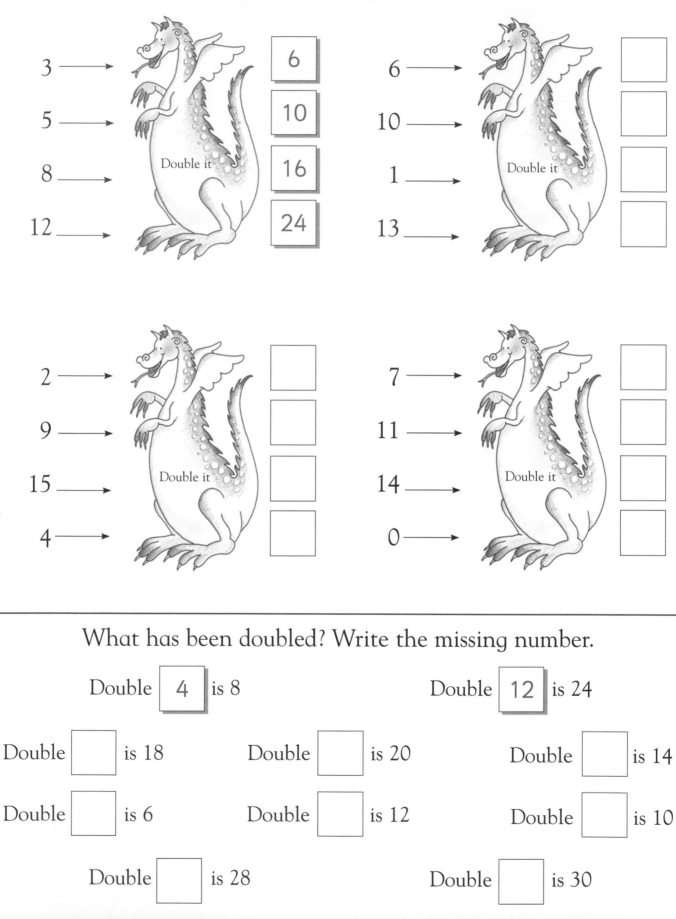

3 → Double it → 6

5 → → 10

8 → → 16

12 → → 24

6 → Double it →

10 → →

1 → →

13 → →

2 → Double it →

9 → →

15 → →

4 → →

7 → Double it →

11 → →

14 → →

0 → →

What has been doubled? Write the missing number.

Double $\boxed{4}$ is 8

Double $\boxed{12}$ is 24

Double $\boxed{}$ is 18

Double $\boxed{}$ is 20

Double $\boxed{}$ is 14

Double $\boxed{}$ is 6

Double $\boxed{}$ is 12

Double $\boxed{}$ is 10

Double $\boxed{}$ is 28

Double $\boxed{}$ is 30

Real-life problems

All the piggy banks need 20p. Draw different coins in each one.
You can use any coin more than once.

Real-life problems

Complete the pictures, then write the sums.

There were 12 biscuits. James ate 3. How many were left?

12 − 3 = 9

Share 12 marbles equally between 3 people. How many marbles will each have?

☐ ÷ ☐ = ☐

Susie has 10 fish. She is given 11 more for her birthday. How many fish does she have altogether?

☐ + ☐ = ☐

Joe had 5 boxes. He had 6 pencils in each box. How many pencils did he have altogether?

☐ x ☐ = ☐

If you share 20 carrots equally between 4 rabbits, how many carrots will each have?

☐ ÷ ☐ = ☐

Mum had 16 cups, but she broke 9. How many cups has she got left?

☐ − ☐ = ☐

Number families

Use the 3 numbers to make 4 different sums.

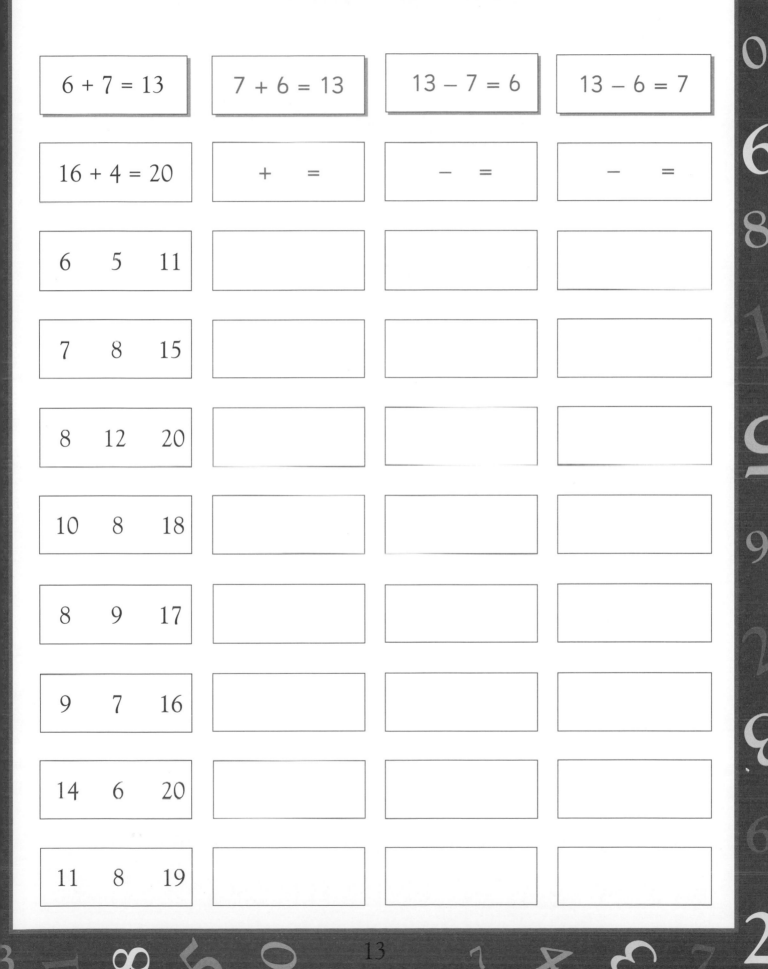

6 + 7 = 13	7 + 6 = 13	13 – 7 = 6	13 – 6 = 7
16 + 4 = 20	+ =	– =	– =
6 5 11			
7 8 15			
8 12 20			
10 8 18			
8 9 17			
9 7 16			
14 6 20			
11 8 19			

Patterns

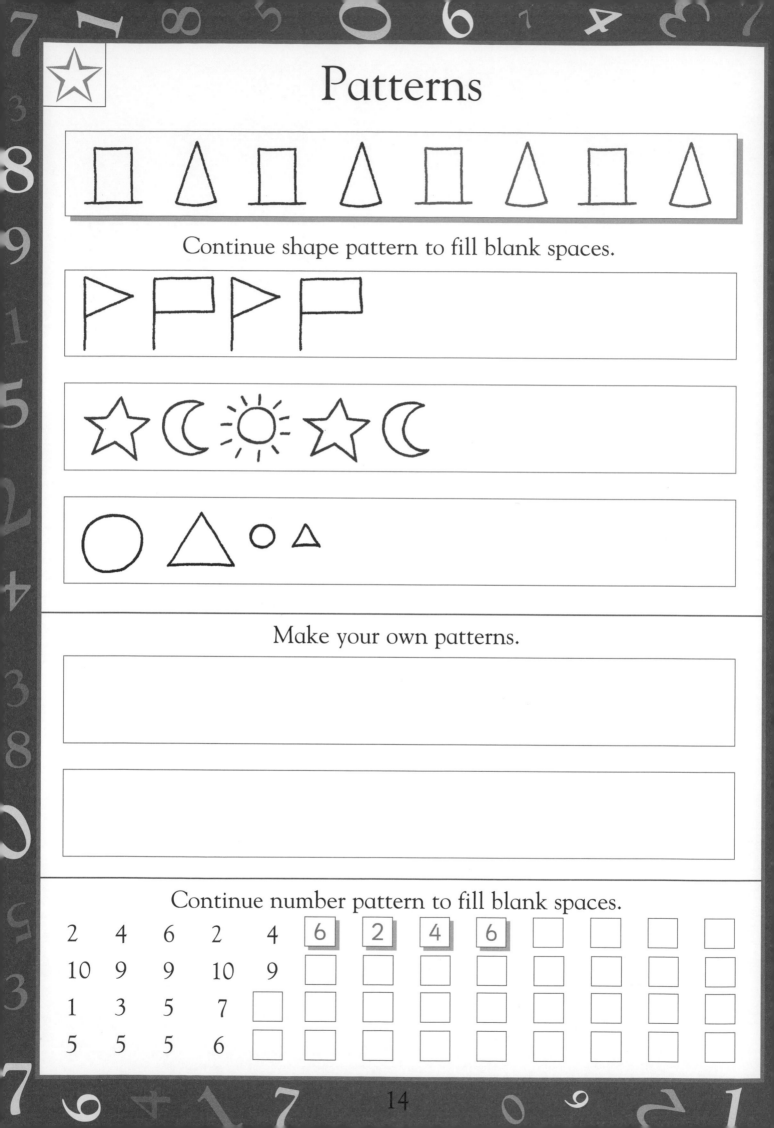

Continue shape pattern to fill blank spaces.

Make your own patterns.

Continue number pattern to fill blank spaces.

2	4	6	2	4	6	2	4	6				
10	9	9	10	9								
1	3	5	7									
5	5	5	6									

3D shapes

cube   cuboid   sphere   pyramid

Match the shapes to the names.

pyramid   sphere   cube   cuboid

How many?   How many?

2

Comparing shapes

How many corners and sides does each shape have?
Remember: Some shapes have no corners or sides.
Some have three, four, or more corners and sides.

4 corners	☐ corners	☐ corners
4 sides	☐ sides	☐ sides

☐ corners	☐ corners	☐ corners
☐ sides	☐ sides	☐ sides

Read the questions and fill in the missing numbers.

How are squares and rectangles alike? They both have ☐ sides and ☐ corners.

How are circles and triangles different?

Triangles have ☐ corners and ☐ sides.

Circles have ☐ corners and ☐ sides.

How are circles and ovals alike? They both have ☐ sides.

Sorting shapes

Circle the shapes that belong in each group.

Shapes with no corners

Shapes with four corners

Write the answer to the mystery sentences.

Janette saw a shape with three sides. It looked like a
slice of pizza. Which shape did she see? ....

Mike saw a shape with four sides. Two sides were short.
The other two sides were longer. Which shape did he see? ....

Peter saw a shape with no sides. It looked like
an egg. Which shape did he see? ....

Using clocks

Circle "yes" or "no" to answer the questions below.

John starts school at 9 o'clock. Does the clock show it is time for John to start school?

Yes   No

Look at the time on the clock. It is time for maths. Does maths start at 10:00?

8:00   Yes   No

Look at the clock. Reading starts in 1 hour. At what time will reading start?

Sam and his mum went to the shop. They left for the shop at 4 o'clock. They arrived back at home at 5 o'clock.

How long were Sam and his mother gone?   1 minute   1 hour

Look at the clock on the right. Lunch will start in half an hour. What time will lunch start?

Differences in time

Circle the activity in each group below that takes more time.

Circle the activity in each group below that takes less time.

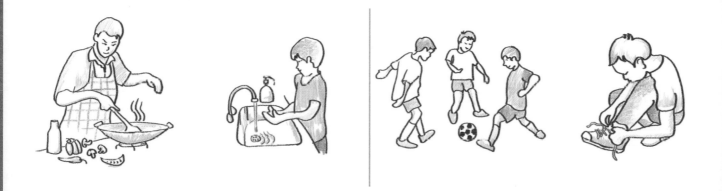

About how long does each activity take? Circle the best answer.

1 minute   1 hour   1 minute   1 hour   1 minute   1 hour

Days of the week

Circle the correct answer for each question below.

Which is the first day of the week?	Sunday	Saturday
Which day comes before Wednesday?	Friday	Tuesday
Which day comes after Sunday?	Monday	Wednesday
Which day comes after Friday?	Tuesday	Saturday

July

Sunday	Monday	Tuesday	Wednesday	Thursday	Friday	Saturday
	1	2	3	4	5	6
7	8	9	10	11	12	13
14	15	16	17	18	19	20
☼ 21	22	23	24	25	26	27
28	29	30	31			

Use the calendar above to answer each question.
Circle your answers.

What day of the week is numbered 1?	Thursday	Monday
What is the second Tuesday numbered?	9	16
Which date shows ☼ ?	12	21
How many days are there in this month?	28	31
How many Sundays are there in this month?	4	5

Months and years

January	February	March	April
31 days	28 days	31 days	30 days

May	June	July	August
31 days	30 days	31 days	31 days

September	October	November	December
30 days	31 days	30 days	31 days

Use the information above to answer each question.

Which month comes after January? ....

Which is the month with the fewest days? ....

How many months begin with the letter J? ☐

How many months have 30 days? ☐

How many months have 31 days? ☐

Which month comes between July and September? ....

Which month comes before June? ....

In the chart above, circle the month of your birthday.

Write the month of your birthday here. ....

How old are you? ☐ years

Comparing

heavier   lighter   bigger smaller   longer   shorter

Draw the pictures and say ...

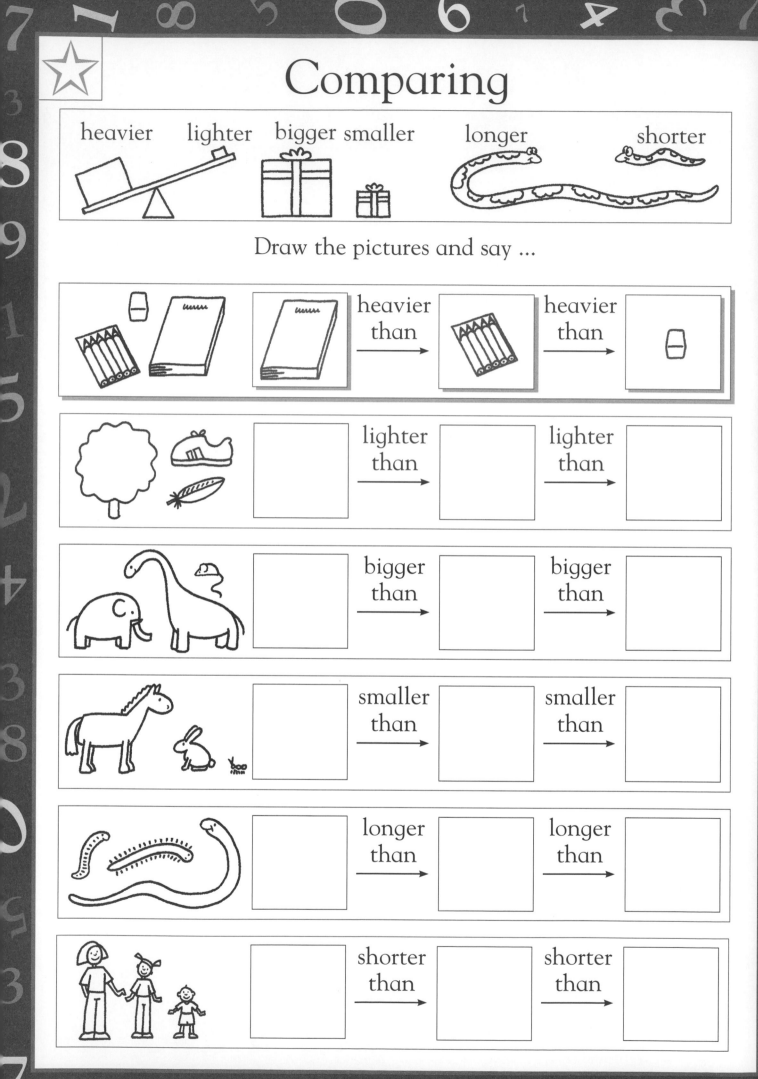

heavier than → heavier than →

lighter than → lighter than →

bigger than → bigger than →

smaller than → smaller than →

longer than → longer than →

shorter than → shorter than →

Length

Each number marks a centimetre.

10 centimetres

Each number marks a centimetre.

5 centimetres

Measure using a 1p coin.

☐ pence long

☐ pence long

Use a ruler to measure this object in centimetres.

☐ centimetres long

Use a ruler to measure this object in centimetres.

☐ centimetres long

Compare sizes

Look at the animals and performers on the paths to the circus tent.

Path 1. Circle the largest.
Path 2. Circle the shortest.

Path 3. Circle the tallest.
Path 4. Circle the smallest.

Read each question, and circle the answer.

Which is heavier?

Which holds more?

Sequence of events

Write B for before and A for after.

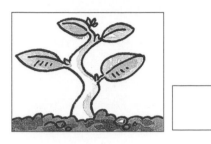 ☐

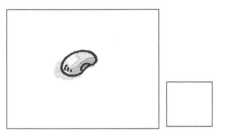 ☐

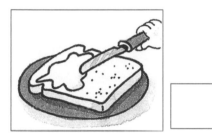 ☐

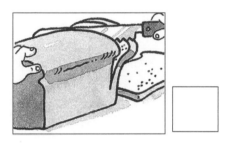 ☐

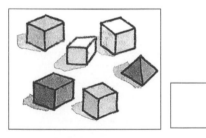 ☐

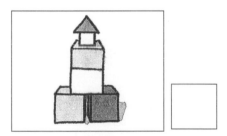 ☐

Look at the pictures below and answer the questions.

morning

afternoon

evening

What happened first? ....

What happened next? ....

What happened last? ....

Quick adding

Practice doing quick addition.

How quickly can you solve these equations? Ready, set, go!

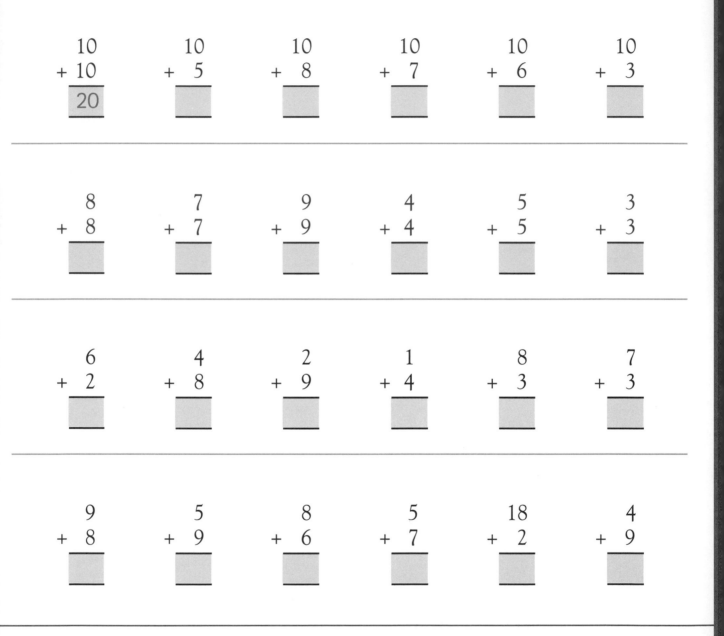

10	10	10	10	10	10
+ 10	+ 5	+ 8	+ 7	+ 6	+ 3
20					

| 8 | 7 | 9 | 4 | 5 | 3 |
| + 8 | + 7 | + 9 | + 4 | + 5 | + 3 |

| 6 | 4 | 2 | 1 | 8 | 7 |
| + 2 | + 8 | + 9 | + 4 | + 3 | + 3 |

| 9 | 5 | 8 | 5 | 18 | 4 |
| + 8 | + 9 | + 6 | + 7 | + 2 | + 9 |

Add the three numbers in each equation.

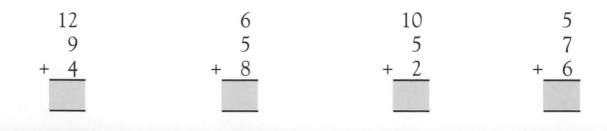

12	6	10	5
9	5	5	7
+ 4	+ 8	+ 2	+ 6

Quick subtracting

Practice doing quick subtraction.

Solve these equations quickly. You can do it!

$6 - 3$	$7 - 3$	$29 - 9$	$9 - 6$	$16 - 8$	$7 - 1$
3					

$10 - 2$	$29 - 7$	$12 - 6$	$16 - 4$	$18 - 10$	$16 - 6$

$18 - 8$	$9 - 5$	$16 - 5$	$17 - 7$	$16 - 3$	$19 - 9$

$14 - 6$	$10 - 6$	$109 - 9$	$47 - 7$	$18 - 9$	$17 - 10$

Circle the number sentence that is related to $10 - 4 = 6$.

$6 - 4 = 2$ $6 + 4 = 10$ $10 + 4 = 14$

Practise subtraction

Practise your subtraction skills.

Subtract and write the answers in each row.

15	29	18	16	12	19
− 4	− 6	− 5	− 4	− 2	− 3
11					

10	9	39	20	16	56
− 7	− 5	− 4	− 10	− 8	− 6

14	9	60	89	18	58
− 7	− 6	− 30	− 9	− 15	− 8

Read each story.
Then write the answer for each subtraction problem.

Juan had thirteen crayons.
He broke two crayons. How many
of his crayons were not broken?

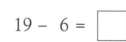

13 − 2 = ☐

We saw twenty-five bunnies.
Four bunnies ran away.
How many bunnies were left?

25 − 4 = ☐

Jen made nineteen cupcakes.
She gave away six cupcakes.
How many cupcakes were left?

19 − 6 = ☐

Graphs

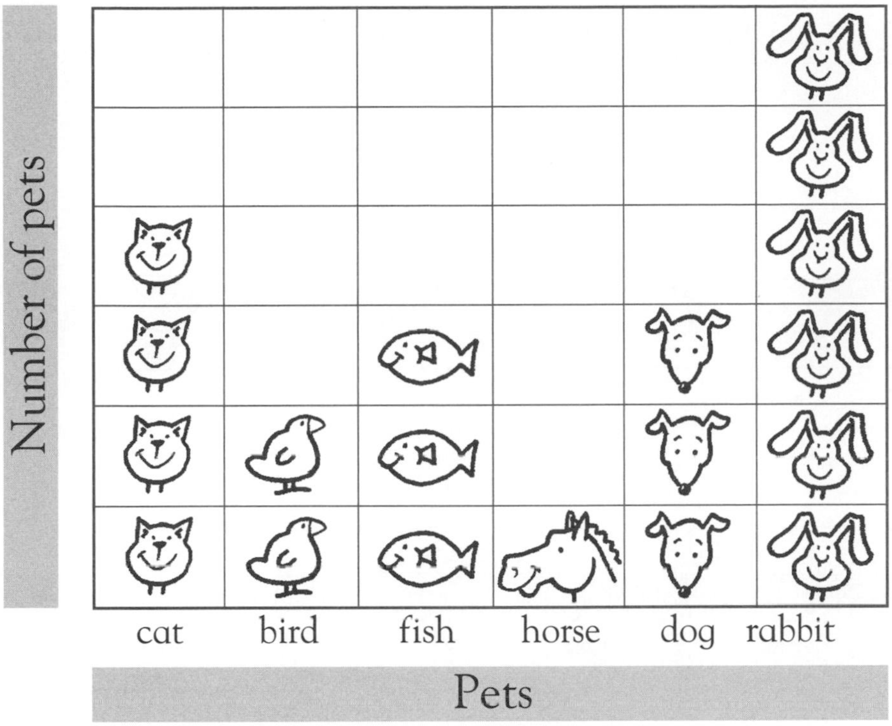

Number of pets

					🐕
					🐕
🐱					🐕
🐱		🐟		🐶	🐕
🐱	🐦	🐟		🐶	🐕
🐱	🐦	🐟	🐴	🐶	🐕
cat	bird	fish	horse	dog	rabbit

Pets

How many pets?

🐱 `4`   🐦 ☐

🐟 ☐   🐴 ☐

🐶 ☐   🐕 ☐

Which pet? 6 [🐰] 2 ☐ 1 ☐

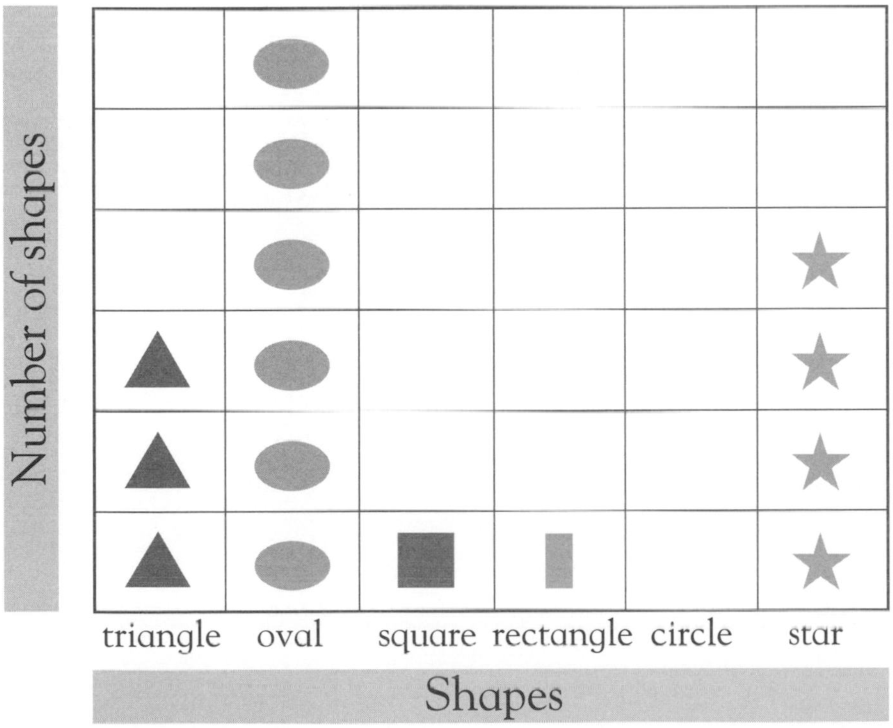

Number of shapes

	⬭				
	⬭				
	⬭				★
▲	⬭				★
▲	⬭				★
▲	⬭	■	▮		★
triangle	oval	square	rectangle	circle	star

Shapes

How many shapes?

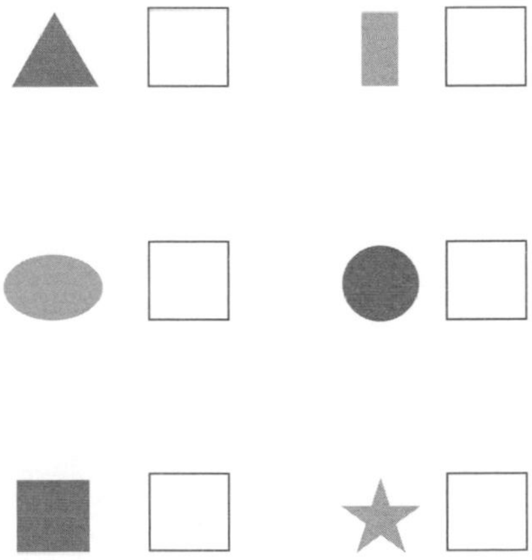

▲ ☐   ▮ ☐

⬭ ☐   ● ☐

■ ☐   ★ ☐

Which shape? 4 ☐ 0 ☐ 3 ☐

Picture graphs

Use this picture graph to answer each question.

Dogs in need of homes

black dogs	🐕 🐕 🐕 🐕
white dogs	🐕 🐕 🐕
spotted dogs	🐕 🐕 🐕
grey dogs	🐕 🐕 🐕 🐕 🐕

How many black
dogs need homes? ☐

How many spotted
dogs need homes? ☐

Which two kinds of dog are
the same in number?

....

Of which kind of dog
is there the most? ....

How many more grey dogs
are there than spotted dogs? ☐

How many black and
white dogs need homes? ☐

How many dogs are
there in all? ☐

Write the subtraction problem and the answer.
There are 15 dogs in all. People take 4 black ☐
dogs home. How many other dogs still need homes?

Bar graphs

The bar graph shows the number of cakes a bakery sold in a day.
Use the bar graph to answer the questions.

Cakes sold in a day

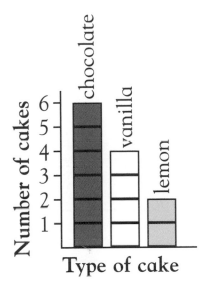

How many lemon
cakes were sold? □

Which cake did the
bakery sell the most of? ....

How many vanilla
cakes were sold? □

The bar graph shows the number of animals that live on
Mr. Jones's farm. Use the bar graph to answer each question.

Animals on Mr. Jones's farm

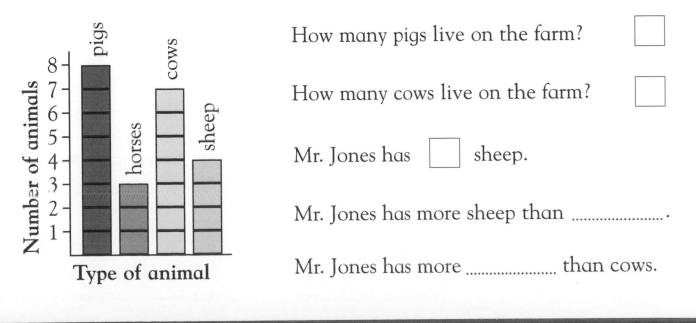

How many pigs live on the farm? □

How many cows live on the farm? □

Mr. Jones has □ sheep.

Mr. Jones has more sheep than ....

Mr. Jones has more .... than cows.

Position words

Follow the directions in each sentence.

Draw a cloud above the rocket.

Draw a sun to the left of the rocket.

Draw a planet to the right of the rocket.

Draw a planet below the rocket.

Circle the correct words to complete the sentences.

The bat is .... the ball.

near   far from

The fence is .... the house.

behind   in front of

The girl is walking ....

up the hill   down the hill

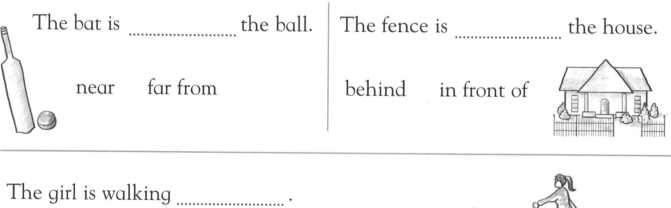

Read the clues, then write each child's name under the correct picture.

Kim is in the middle.
Tom is to the right of Kim.
Bill is to the left of Kim.

....

Answer Section with Parents' Notes

Key Stage 1
Ages 5–6
Advanced

This 8-page section provides answers to all the activities in the book. This will enable you to mark your child's work or can be used by them if they prefer to do their own marking.

The notes for each page help explain the common pitfalls and problems and, where appropriate, give indications as to what practice is needed to ensure children understand where they have gone wrong.

Numbers

Which numbers are the snakes hiding?
Look, and say them as you write.

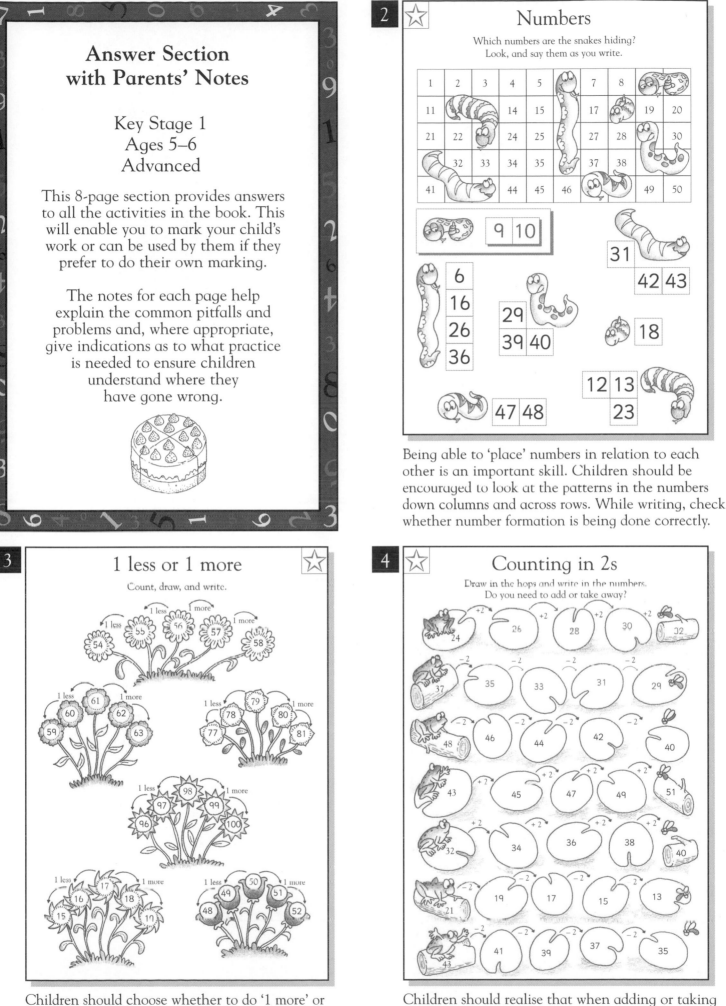

Being able to 'place' numbers in relation to each other is an important skill. Children should be encouraged to look at the patterns in the numbers down columns and across rows. While writing, check whether number formation is being done correctly.

1 less or 1 more

Count, draw, and write.

Children should choose whether to do '1 more' or '1 less' first. Do they realise that they are taking away (or adding) one each time? Children often find it tricky when numbers 'cross a ten', e.g. 79. Practice with small numbers will help.

Counting in 2s

Draw in the hops and write in the numbers.
Do you need to add or take away?

Children should realise that when adding or taking away two, if they begin with an odd number they will end with an odd number, and vice versa. They can use this information to check their answers and add or subtract two from any other number.

Counting in 3s, 4s, and 5s

Draw in the arrows and write the numbers on the toadstools.
Do you need to add or take away?

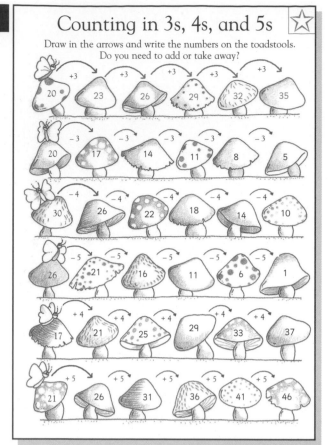

Can children now 'picture' 3 more, or 4 less, in their minds without fingers or other aids? Try to help them realise that +3 is the opposite of -3. Having moved from 20 to 5 in steps of 3, can they get back to 20 again? (They need to +3 the same number of times.)

Patterns of 2, 5, and 10

Count, colour, and find a pattern.

Count in 2s and colour them red.

1	2	3	4	5	6	7	8	9	10
11	12	13	14	15	16	17	18	19	20
21	22	23	24	25	26	27	28	29	30
31	32	33	34	35	36	37	38	39	40
41	42	43	44	45	46	47	48	49	50

Count in 5s and colour them purple.

1	2	3	4	5	6	7	8	9	10
11	12	13	14	15	16	17	18	19	20
21	22	23	24	25	26	27	28	29	30
31	32	33	34	35	36	37	38	39	40
41	42	43	44	45	46	47	48	49	50

Count in 10s and colour them yellow.

1	2	3	4	5	6	7	8	9	10
11	12	13	14	15	16	17	18	19	20
21	22	23	24	25	26	27	28	29	30
31	32	33	34	35	36	37	38	39	40
41	42	43	44	45	46	47	48	49	50

Discuss the patterns made. Are there any numbers that are coloured in all the patterns? (The 10s will be.) Why is this? Help children see that all the multiples of 5 end in a 5 or a 0.

More or less

Link the spaceships to the planets, and the rockets to the stars.

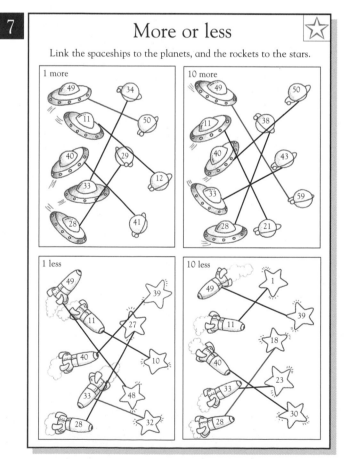

Discuss the changes happening to each set of numbers. Is it the tens or the units digit that changes? Is '10 more' the same as adding or taking away 10? Do the numbers always get larger or smaller when finding '10 less'?

Fractions of numbers

Draw a ring round the objects that make up the fractions and write the missing numbers.

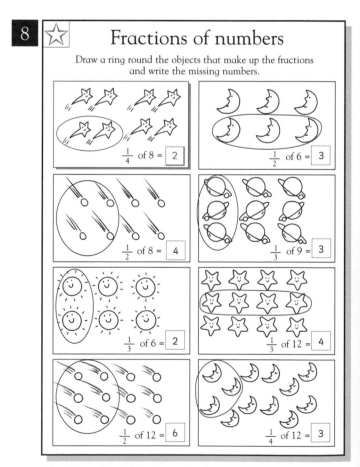

$\frac{1}{4}$ of 8 = 2

$\frac{1}{2}$ of 6 = 3

$\frac{1}{2}$ of 8 = 4

$\frac{1}{3}$ of 9 = 3

$\frac{1}{3}$ of 6 = 2

$\frac{1}{3}$ of 12 = 4

$\frac{1}{2}$ of 12 = 6

$\frac{1}{4}$ of 12 = 3

Children should look at the bottom number of the fraction (denominator) to check how many groups the set should be split into. ($\frac{1}{3}$ will need three groups.) You can try extending to questions like 'if one-third of the stars is 4, how many would be in two-thirds?'

Adding grid

Draw rings round the pairs of numbers that add up to 20.

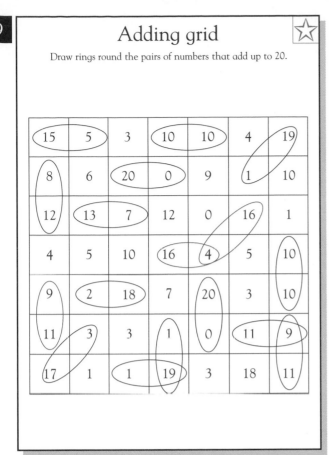

If children find this page difficult, it would be worth finding 20 objects, such as pencils or pasta shapes and finding different ways of splitting them into 2 piles, e.g. 2 18, 15 and 5. Children can then look for these pairs of numbers.

Doubles

Write the missing numbers.

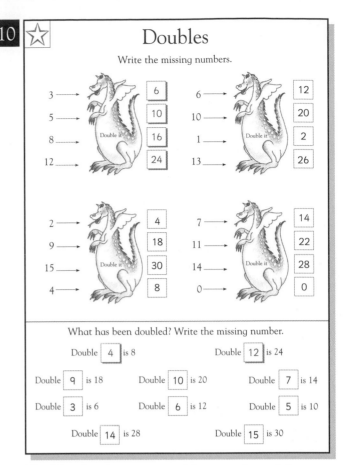

What has been doubled? Write the missing number.

Double 4 is 8   Double 12 is 24

Double 9 is 18   Double 10 is 20   Double 7 is 14

Double 3 is 6   Double 6 is 12   Double 5 is 10

Double 14 is 28   Double 15 is 30

'Doubling' is the same as adding two lots of the same number. If children cannot yet double in their heads, use pasta shapes to make two piles of the number and add them to help with initial calculations. Children should aim to memorise answers.

Real-life problems

All the piggy banks need 20p. Draw different coins in each one.
You can use any coin more than once.

Explain that to make 5p, five 1p coins, or 2p, 2p, 1p, or 2p, 1p, 1p, 1p, or a 5p coin on its own can be used. So 10p can be made with any of these combinations plus a 5p coin, then another 10p coin will make 20p.

Real-life problems

Complete the pictures, then write the sums.

There were 12 biscuits. James ate 3. How many were left?

12 − 3 = 9

Share 12 marbles equally between 3 people. How many marbles will each have?

12 ÷ 3 = 4

Susie has 10 fish. She is given 11 more for her birthday. How many fish does she have altogether?

10 + 11 = 21

Joe had 5 boxes. He had 6 pencils in each box. How many pencils did he have altogether?

6 x 5 = 30

If you share 20 carrots equally between 4 rabbits, how many carrots will each have?

20 ÷ 4 = 5

Mum had 16 cups, but she broke 9. How many cups has she got left?

16 − 9 = 7

When drawing, children should work out the operation they need, and which quantity is being shared or taken away. Do they know that in addition 4+5 and 5+4, or in multiplication 6*10 and 10*6, are the same, but that subtraction and division do not work the same way?

13 — Number families

Use the 3 numbers to make 4 different sums.

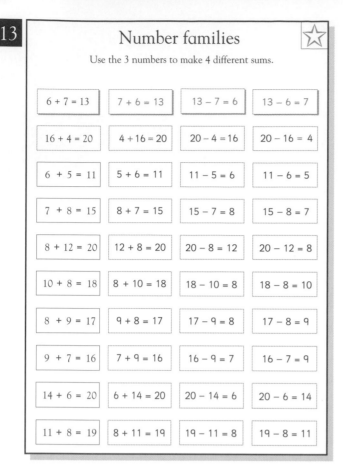

6 + 7 = 13	7 + 6 = 13	13 – 7 = 6	13 – 6 = 7
16 + 4 = 20	4 + 16 = 20	20 – 4 = 16	20 – 16 = 4
6 + 5 = 11	5 + 6 = 11	11 – 5 = 6	11 – 6 = 5
7 + 8 = 15	8 + 7 = 15	15 – 7 = 8	15 – 8 = 7
8 + 12 = 20	12 + 8 = 20	20 – 8 = 12	20 – 12 = 8
10 + 8 = 18	8 + 10 = 18	18 – 10 = 8	18 – 8 = 10
8 + 9 = 17	9 + 8 = 17	17 – 9 = 8	17 – 8 = 9
9 + 7 = 16	7 + 9 = 16	16 – 9 = 7	16 – 7 = 9
14 + 6 = 20	6 + 14 = 20	20 – 14 = 6	20 – 6 = 14
11 + 8 = 19	8 + 11 = 19	19 – 11 = 8	19 – 8 = 11

This activity will help children see that if they know one combination of the numbers, then they really do know three other versions as well. If they know that 6+7=13 then, with a little practice, they will readily be able to give the answers to 7+6, 13-6, and 13-7.

14 — Patterns

Continue shape pattern to fill blank spaces.

Make your own patterns.

Answers may vary

Answers may vary

Continue number pattern to fill blank spaces.

2	4	6	2	4	6	2	4	6	2	4	6	2
10	9	9	10	9	9	10	9	9	10	9	9	10
1	3	5	7	1	3	5	7	1	3	5	7	1
5	5	5	6	5	5	5	6	5	5	5	6	5

Encourage the child to talk about their own patterns and to explain what they have done. Explain that in a mathematical pattern things repeat in a predictable way. There is more than one way for the last patterns to be repeated.

15 — 3D shapes

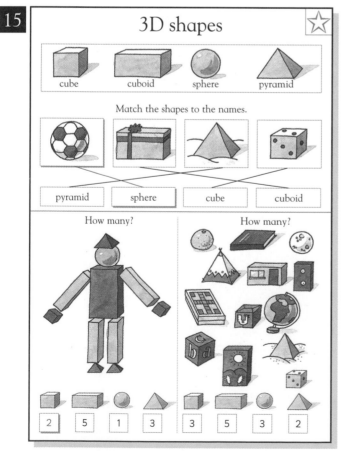

cube   cuboid   sphere   pyramid

Match the shapes to the names.

pyramid   sphere   cube   cuboid

How many?

2   5   1   3

How many?

3   5   3   2

Can the child hunt around their toy box or a food cupboard to find real-life examples of these shapes? Check that they recognise the same shapes positioned differently. For instance, do they recognise a pyramid standing on its point?

16 — Comparing shapes

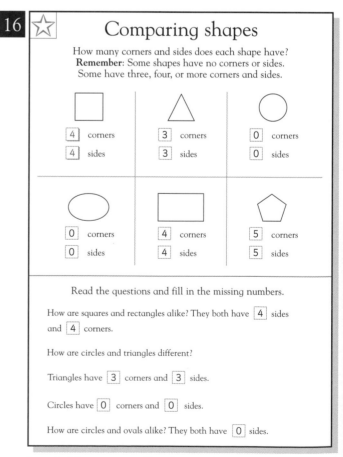

How many corners and sides does each shape have?
Remember: Some shapes have no corners or sides. Some have three, four, or more corners and sides.

4 corners	3 corners	0 corners
4 sides	3 sides	0 sides
0 corners	4 corners	5 corners
0 sides	4 sides	5 sides

Read the questions and fill in the missing numbers.

How are squares and rectangles alike? They both have 4 sides and 4 corners.

How are circles and triangles different?

Triangles have 3 corners and 3 sides.

Circles have 0 corners and 0 sides.

How are circles and ovals alike? They both have 0 sides.

Let children create flat shapes from modeling clay. Ask them to make at least three of each shape on the page, each one a different size. Then have children order the three clay versions of each shape by size, either from largest to smallest or from smallest to largest.

Sorting shapes

Circle the shapes that belong in each group.

Shapes with no corners

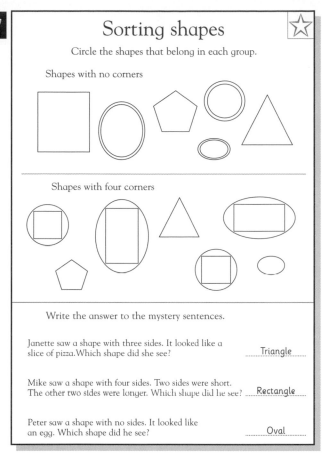

Shapes with four corners

Write the answer to the mystery sentences.

Janette saw a shape with three sides. It looked like a slice of pizza. Which shape did she see? ...... Triangle

Mike saw a shape with four sides. Two sides were short. The other two sides were longer. Which shape did he see? ...... Rectangle

Peter saw a shape with no sides. It looked like an egg. Which shape did he see? ...... Oval

Help children find pictures of objects with the shape of a circle, rectangle, square, oval, and triangle in a magazine. Assist them with cutting out several pictures of each shape. Then let children sort the pictures into groups by shape and create a shape poster.

Using clocks

Circle "yes" or "no" to answer the questions below.

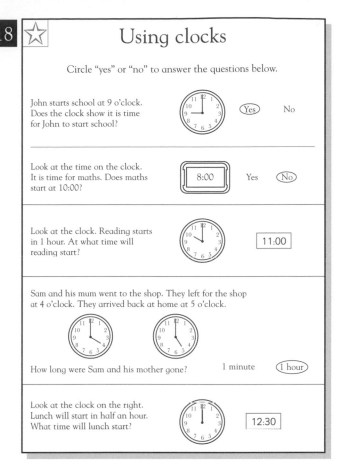

John starts school at 9 o'clock. Does the clock show it is time for John to start school?   (Yes)   No

Look at the time on the clock. It is time for maths. Does maths start at 10:00?   8:00   Yes   (No)

Look at the clock. Reading starts in 1 hour. At what time will reading start?   11:00

Sam and his mum went to the shop. They left for the shop at 4 o'clock. They arrived back at home at 5 o'clock.

How long were Sam and his mother gone?   1 minute   (1 hour)

Look at the clock on the right. Lunch will start in half an hour. What time will lunch start?   12:30

Draw analogue and digital clock faces, showing times on the hour and on the half hour, on index cards. Mix the cards, and let children sort the cards to match the analogue clock time with its corresponding digital time.

Differences in time

Circle the activity in each group below that takes more time.

Circle the activity in each group below that takes less time.

About how long does each activity take? Circle the best answer.

1 minute (1 hour)   (1 minute) 1 hour   (1 minute) 1 hour

Discuss various other activities with children, and let them give an appropriate time it might take to perform each one. As children practise assessing differences in time duration, they will become increasingly competent at judging lengths of time.

Days of the week

Circle the correct answer for each question below.

Which is the first day of the week?   (Sunday)   Saturday

Which day comes before Wednesday?   Friday   (Tuesday)

Which day comes after Sunday?   (Monday)   Wednesday

Which day comes after Friday?   Tuesday   (Saturday)

July

Sunday	Monday	Tuesday	Wednesday	Thursday	Friday	Saturday
	1	2	3	4	5	6
7	8	9	10	11	12	13
14	15	16	17	18	19	20
☼21	22	23	24	25	26	27
28	29	30	31			

Use the calendar above to answer each question. Circle your answers.

What day of the week is numbered 1?   Thursday   (Monday)

What is the second Tuesday numbered?   (9)   16

Which date shows ☼ ?   12   (21)

How many days are there in this month?   28   (31)

How many Sundays are there in this month?   (4)   5

For additional practice, say the name of a day of the week, then ask children to name the day that comes either before it or after it. Let children check their answers by looking at a calendar.

Months and years

January 31 days	February 28 days	March 31 days	April 30 days
May 31 days	June 30 days	July 31 days	August 31 days
September 30 days	October 31 days	November 30 days	December 31 days

Use the information above to answer each question.

Which month comes after January? ...... February

Which is the month with the fewest days? ...... February

How many months begin with the letter J? [3]

How many months have 30 days? [4]

How many months have 31 days? [7]

Which month comes between July and September? ...... August

Which month comes before June? ...... May

In the chart above, circle the month of your birthday.

Write the month of your birthday here. ....

How old are you? [ ] years

Answers may vary

Have children repeat after you the names of the months of the year. Then talk about the weather where you live; let them choose different months and draw pictures to show what the weather is typically like during each of those months.

Comparing

heavier   lighter   bigger   smaller   longer   shorter

Draw the pictures and say ...

If your child experiences difficulty in comparing three objects, let them try actually holding pairs of household objects. Encourage them to compare these side by side and to get used to using the language involved before comparing the sets of three objects.

Length

Each number marks a centimetre.

10 centimetres

Each number marks a centimetre.

5 centimetres

Measure using a 1 p coin.

[4] pence long

[2] pence long

Use a ruler to measure this object in centimetres.

[10] centimetres long

Use a ruler to measure this object in centimetres.

[8] centimetres long

Let children practice measuring straight objects using a ruler. Help them understand where each centimetre mark appears on the ruler. Have children write down the measurements, using the word 'centimetre'.

Compare sizes

Look at the animals and performers on the paths to the circus tent.

Path 1. Circle the largest.   **Path 3.** Circle the tallest.
Path 2. Circle the shortest.   **Path 4.** Circle the smallest.

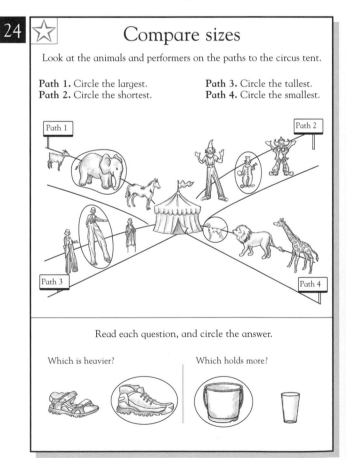

Read each question, and circle the answer.

Which is heavier?   Which holds more?

Show children hats, mittens, or boxes of different sizes. Let them indicate which is biggest or smallest, widest, thinnest, and so on. Do the same with other objects, letting children order them from smallest to largest.

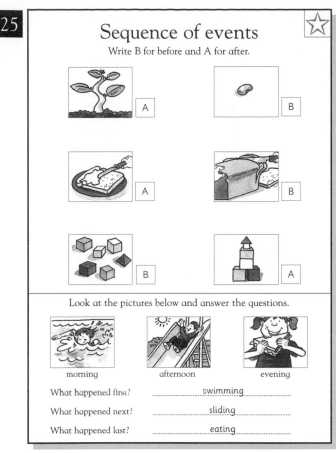

Sequence of events

Write B for before and A for after.

Look at the pictures below and answer the questions.

morning   afternoon   evening

What happened first? .... swimming ....

What happened next? .... sliding ....

What happened last? .... eating ....

Even more important than the order chosen by the child will be their reasons for so choosing and their ability to discuss these. It will help to relate the pictures to events in the child's own day and to the order in which things happen.

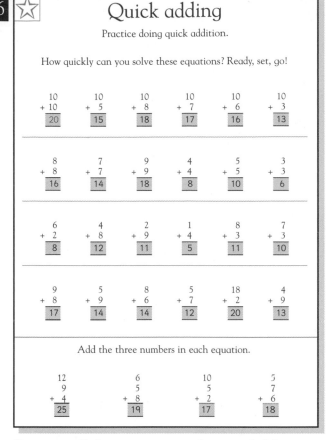

Quick adding

Practice doing quick addition.

How quickly can you solve these equations? Ready, set, go!

10 +10 = 20	10 +5 = 15	10 +8 = 18	10 +7 = 17	10 +6 = 16	10 +3 = 13
8 +8 = 16	7 +7 = 14	9 +9 = 18	4 +4 = 8	5 +5 = 10	3 +3 = 6
6 +2 = 8	4 +8 = 12	2 +9 = 11	1 +4 = 5	8 +3 = 11	7 +3 = 10
9 +8 = 17	5 +9 = 14	8 +6 = 14	5 +7 = 12	18 +2 = 20	4 +9 = 13

Add the three numbers in each equation.

12 9 +4 = 25   6 5 +8 = 19   10 5 +2 = 17   5 7 +6 = 18

Covering all the rows, except the one children are currently working on, to help them avoid losing their place. Help them learn quick addition facts through frequent practice, using flash cards or items such as marbles, paper clips, and blocks.

Quick subtracting

Practice doing quick subtraction.

Solve these equations quickly. You can do it!

6 -3 = 3	7 -3 = 4	29 -9 = 20	9 -6 = 3	16 -8 = 8	7 -1 = 6
10 -2 = 8	29 -7 = 22	12 -6 = 6	16 -4 = 12	18 -10 = 8	16 -6 = 10
18 -8 = 10	9 -5 = 4	16 -5 = 11	17 -7 = 10	16 -3 = 13	19 -9 = 10
14 -6 = 8	10 -6 = 4	109 -9 = 100	47 -7 = 40	18 -9 = 9	17 -10 = 7

Circle the number sentence that is related to 10 - 4 = 6.

6 - 4 = 2   (6 + 4 = 10)   10 + 4 = 14

Again, cover all the rows children are not currently working on, to help them keep their concentration. Frequent practice, using flash cards or manipulative items, is important for them to become quick at working out subtraction equations.

Practise subtraction

Practise your subtraction skills.

Subtract and write the answers in each row.

15 -4 = 11	29 -6 = 23	18 -5 = 13	16 -4 = 12	12 -2 = 10	19 -3 = 16
10 -7 = 3	9 -5 = 4	39 -4 = 35	20 -10 = 10	16 -8 = 8	56 -6 = 50
14 -7 = 7	9 -6 = 3	60 -30 = 30	89 -9 = 80	18 -15 = 3	58 -8 = 50

Read each story.
Then write the answer for each subtraction problem.

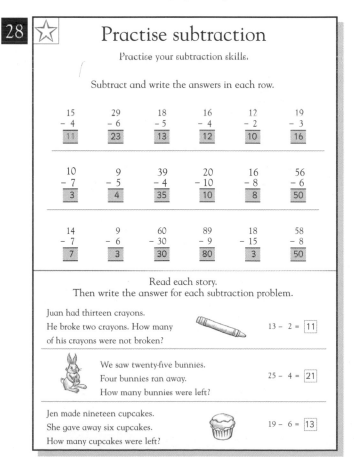

Juan had thirteen crayons. He broke two crayons. How many of his crayons were not broken?   13 - 2 = 11

We saw twenty-five bunnies. Four bunnies ran away. How many bunnies were left?   25 - 4 = 21

Jen made nineteen cupcakes. She gave away six cupcakes. How many cupcakes were left?   19 - 6 = 13

Write subtraction problems on up to twenty index cards. Write an answer for each problem on another index card. Place all the cards on a table face up. Let children match a problem card with the correct answer card.

29 ☆ Graphs

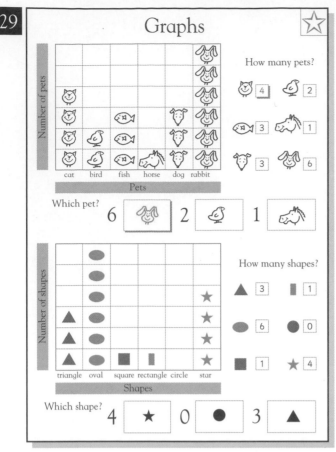

How many pets?

🐱 4   🐦 2
🐟 3   🐴 1
🐕 3   🐰 6

Which pet?

6 🐕   2 🐦   1 🐴

How many shapes?

▲ 3   ▮ 1
⬭ 6   ● 0
■ 1   ★ 4

Which shape?

4 ★   0 ●   3 ▲

Before tackling the questions, encourage the child to talk about the graph and all that it shows. What is the hightest number? (6). How many different types of pets are there across the graph? (6).

30 ☆ Picture graphs

Use this picture graph to answer each question.

Dogs in need of homes

black dogs	🐕 🐕 🐕 🐕
white dogs	🐕 🐕 🐕
spotted dogs	🐕 🐕 🐕
grey dogs	🐕 🐕 🐕 🐕 🐕

How many black dogs need homes? 4

How many spotted dogs need homes? 3

Which two kinds of dog are the same in number?
white dogs and spotted dogs

Of which kind of dog is there the most? _grey dogs_

How many more grey dogs are there than spotted dogs? 2

How many black and white dogs need homes? 7

How many dogs are there in all? 15

Write the subtraction problem and the answer. There are 15 dogs in all. People take 4 black dogs home. How many other dogs still need homes? 15 − 4 = 11

Help children understand that each picture graph stands for one object. Show them how to count each object in each row. When children understand this concept, ask questions like, "How many more black dogs than white dogs are there?"

31 Bar graphs ☆

The bar graph shows the number of cakes a bakery sold in a day. Use the bar graph to answer the questions.

Cakes sold in a day

How many lemon cakes were sold? 2

Which cake did the bakery sell the most of? _chocolate_

How many vanilla cakes were sold? 4

The bar graph shows the number of animals that live on Mr. Jones's farm. Use the bar graph to answer each question.

Animals on Mr. Jones's farm

How many pigs live on the farm? 8

How many cows live on the farm? 7

Mr. Jones has 4 sheep.

Mr. Jones has more sheep than _horses_ .

Mr. Jones has more _pigs_ than cows.

Explain to children that each box on the bar graph stands for one object. They can count the boxes in each bar to find the answers to the questions on this page.

32 ☆ Position words

Follow the directions in each sentence.

Draw a cloud above the rocket.

Draw a sun to the left of the rocket.

Draw a planet to the right of the rocket.

Draw a planet below the rocket.

Circle the correct words to complete the sentences.

The bat is _____ the ball.
(near)   far from

The fence is _____ the house.
behind   (in front of)

The girl is walking _____ .
(up the hill)   down the hill

Read the clues, then write each child's name under the correct picture.

Kim is in the middle.
Tom is to the right of Kim.
Bill is to the left of Kim.

Bill   Kim   Tom

Write position words – such as 'behind', 'near', 'next to', 'to the left of', etc. – on index cards. Let children choose a card and use its word or phrase to describe where objects in the home are located in relation to other objects.